PLATE I (*Frontispiece*)

IN THE NORTH SEA
Lewis Gunner on Trawler Mine-Sweeper ready for action.

ANTI-AIRCRAFT DEFENCE

Against

LOW-FLYING ENEMY AIRCRAFT

A Handbook for Light Machine-Gunners

INCLUDING PARTICULARS OF NOTABLE SUCCESSES IN
RECENT FIGHTING BY LAND AND SEA

By

MAJOR C. H. B. PRIDHAM

The Duke of Wellington's Regt.
(Late Officer-Instructor, School of Musketry, Hythe.)
Author of " Lewis Gun Mechanism Made Easy."

ILLUSTRATED WITH PLATES AND DIAGRAMS

The Naval & Military Press Ltd

Published by

The Naval & Military Press Ltd
Unit 5 Riverside, Brambleside
Bellbrook Industrial Estate
Uckfield, East Sussex
TN22 1QQ England

Tel: +44 (0)1825 749494

www.naval-military-press.com
www.nmarchive.com

PREFACE

In this Handbook for Light Machine-Gunners are set out the first principles of how to engage Low-Flying Enemy Aircraft.

At heights above 1,000 feet hostile aircraft are adequately dealt with in daylight by our Fighter Squadrons and Anti-Aircraft Artillery.

The efficiency of our A-A gun-fire from Warships or Land Batteries, together with the deterring effect of Balloon Barrages, compels Enemy Bombers, and Fighter-Bombers, to fly at heights from which they are unable to aim their bombs with accuracy.

The Dive-Bomber, however, diving down to within about 500 feet of its objective, constitutes a problem that can only be countered effectively by fire from Light Machine-Guns and Rifles.

The recognised principles of A-A Fire Control (as applicable to all Small Arms) are here arranged in a clear and concise manner, calculated to:—

SAVE TIME IN TRAINING

for all personnel manning Light Machine-Guns in Naval Craft, Mine-Sweepers, Trawlers, or A-A units of the Regular Army, the Pioneer Corps and the HOME GUARD.

The instances given (on pages 15–19) of Lewis and Bren Guns *used singly* with notable success against enemy Dive-Bombers in France, during the Dunkirk Evacuation, and in repelling attacks on our Fishing Trawlers, have been selected from reports issued from time to time by the Ministry of Information.

CONTENTS

I

LEWIS GUN NOTES

1. Originally introduced into the British Army (during the War of 1915–18) to supplement the fire power of Infantry Platoons in engaging Ground Targets; Lewis Guns are now used mainly as weapons of A-A Defence—both ashore and afloat—against Low-Flying Enemy Aircraft.

FIRST INTRODUCED

2. Against *Ground Targets*, short bursts of fire of about 10 rounds are sufficient for good fire effect, a fresh aim being taken after each burst to ensure accuracy and fire control.

GROUND TARGETS

3. For *A-A Defence*, however, short bursts of fire are ineffective, and continuous fire is essential. With its special system of Air Cooling (see Section II), the .303 Lewis Gun is capable of sustained fire to a greater degree than other Air Cooled Automatics, and is thus well suited for use against Air Targets.

AIR TARGETS

4. The *L.G. Ring Foresight* (as formerly fitted to Lewis Guns) was designed at a time when the maximum speed of Aircraft did not exceed 150 miles per hour. It provided for a "lead" of 6 degrees, which was the Angle of Deflection available to engage a Target crossing the Gun's position at that speed.

L.G. RING FORESIGHT

ANGLE OF DEFLECTION.

5. The Speed of Aircraft now averages around 300 miles per hour (Fighters very considerably more, Bombers somewhat less). It follows, therefore, that the Angle of Deflection necessary to engage Targets crossing at right angles to the Line of Fire has approximately doubled—viz. to 12 *degrees.*

SPEED OF AIRCRAFT

6. The L.G. Ring Foresight has thus become obsolete. Moreover, it has been found to be impracticable to align sights on Crossing Targets moving at top speeds within effective range.

OBSOLETE SIGHTS

7. *Aiming and Fire Control* are now carried out by the "hosepipe" method of Continuous Fire, aided by Observation of Tracers (see Section V).

FIRE CONTROL BY "HOSE-PIPE"

PARTICULARS OF THE .303 LEWIS (LIGHT MACHINE) GUN

The LEWIS GUN is AIR cooled, GAS operated, and MAGAZINE fed (by circular rotating steel Drums, made to hold 47 rounds*).

WEIGHT OF GUN	.. ..	26 lb.
WEIGHT OF BIPOD	.. ..	2¼ lb.
WEIGHT OF MAGAZINE (empty)	.. ..	1¼ lb.
(full)	.. ..	4¼ lb.
LENGTH OF GUN	.. ..	50¼ in.
LENGTH OF BARREL..	.. .. ..	26¼ in.
RATE OF FIRE (Normal)†	.. 10	rounds per second.

3 to 4 Magazines (about 150 rounds) per minute.

COOLING SYSTEM

The Barrel is in close contact, throughout its length, with an **Aluminium Radiator Casing.** The action of the Gases—concentrated in the Barrel Mouthpiece, and from thence striking against the Fore Radiator Casing—creates a vacuum and consequent suction, which draws **a continual current of cool air through the Flanges of the Radiator, thus rapidly expelling the heat from the Barrel.**

NO BARREL CHANGING IS NECESSARY

MULTIPLE LEWIS GUNS

In order to ensure an even greater volume of fire for A-A purposes, Lewis Guns are also used in Naval Craft, mounted in pairs or in multiple form (see Plate II (A) facing page 6) to engage enemy Dive-Bombers attacking Convoys, etc.

* N.B.—Magazines to hold 94 rounds are also in use. The design of the rotating drum enables it to be enlarged to double the normal size. This increases the value of this Gun for use against Air Targets.

† Lewis Guns have been speeded up for Air Fighting (mounted in Aircraft), to about double the normal Rate of Fire—viz. to 20 rounds per second (equivalent to over 1,100 rounds per minute).

PLATE II (A)

MULTIPLE LEWIS GUNS IN H.M.'S MOTOR TORPEDO BOATS
The Guns are fired in pairs—right and left—with a second pair (underneath)
in reserve.

PLATE II (B)

ROYAL AIR FORCE TYPE OF LEWIS GUN
Mounted in launches used for rescue work at sea. Note Double-
sized Magazine. (See footnote on p. 6.)

METHOD OF HOLDING LEWIS GUN
(For A-A FIRING)

When fixed on A-A Mounting (Folding Tripod or Vertical Pillar).

A.—Held down against Hip with Butt under right arm, by left hand pressing down on small of Butt. Sights cannot be used, and Elevation and Point of Aim must be judged. **BUTT AGAINST HIP**

B.—Held to the Shoulder, permitting use of Sights. **BUTT IN SHOULDER**

N.B.—**LOOSE HOLDING reduces Accuracy in Firing.** **LOOSE HOLDING**

III

PARTICULARS OF THE .300 (AMERICAN TYPE) LEWIS GUN
(As issued to the Home Guard)

The .300 calibre LEWIS GUNS (purchased from the U.S.A.) are as used by the U.S. Air Force, mounted in Aircraft. Being cooled by the passage of the Plane through the air, no system of Air Cooling was necessary. These Guns were therefore not fitted with the Aluminium Radiator and Radiator Casing.

This results in a considerable reduction in Weight, the .300 Lewis weighing about 17 lb. as compared with the 26 lb. of the .303 Gun. **WEIGHT OF THE .300 LEWIS**

Deprived of its Cooling System, however, the .300 Gun is consequently not so well suited for A-A firing as the .303 pattern. *Its normal Rate of Fire is in Short Bursts.* **NO COOLING SYSTEM**

Enemy Aircraft, however—when diving down to attack troops on the move, or other military objectives—are Fleeting Targets presenting themselves for a few seconds only at a time. On such occasions—

"**All units must protect themselves with the weapons at their disposal.**"

It may be necessary, therefore, to use the .300 Lewis to engage such Air Targets.

MINOR VARIATIONS FROM THE .303 GUN

In addition to the above mentioned main difference from the .303 Lewis, the .300 type has certain minor variations, as follows:—

COCKING HANDLE

(1) *The Cocking Handle* is fitted on the left-hand side of the Body.

PINION

(2) *The Pinion* is painted with a red band to distinguish it from that of the .303 Gun. They are not interchangeable.

TRIGGER GROUP

(3) *The Trigger Spring* is fitted to the Sear, and not to the Trigger itself, as in the .303 Gun.

GAS REGULATOR

(4) *The Gas Regulator* has *four* holes (Nos. 1, 2, 3, and 4), varying in size. That of the .303 Gun has two holes only.

The smallest hole that gives sufficient Gas should be used.

GAS CHAMBER GLAND

(5) The Gas Chamber has also a Gas Chamber Gland.

IV

BREN GUN NOTES

ORIGIN

The Bren Gun (name formed from **BR**NO, in Czechoslovakia, where it was first invented, and from **EN**FIELD, where it was subsequently made and perfected), has superseded the Lewis Gun in the British Army as a Platoon Light Automatic for use against Ground and Air Targets.

The Bren is GAS operated, and MAGAZINE fed (with 30 rounds vertically fixed above the Body).

COOLING SYSTEM

COOLING is by AIR, aided by the composition of the Barrel.

A-A MOUNTING

The Bren Tripod can be quickly adapted into an A-A Mounting for use against Low-Flying Enemy Aircraft.

PARTICULARS OF THE .303 BREN (LIGHT MACHINE) GUN

WEIGHT OF GUN (with BIPOD) .. .. 23 lb.
WEIGHT OF SPARE BARREL .. .. 6 lb.
WEIGHT OF MAGAZINE (Filled) .. .. $2\frac{3}{4}$ lb.
WEIGHT OF TRIPOD .. .. .. 30 lb.
LENGTH OF GUN .. .. $45\frac{1}{2}$ in.
LENGTH OF BARREL .. .. .. 25 in.
RATE OF FIRE (Normal) .. 30 rounds
(1 MAG. per minute
RATE OF FIRE (Emergency) .. 120 rounds
(4 MAGS. per minute)
SINGLE SHOTS (by moving lever to "R". can also be fired, if required.

THE BARREL MUST BE CHANGED after firing **CHANGING**
300 rounds (10 Magazines), at the Emergency Rate. **THE**
The Barrel can be changed in approximately 6 seconds. **BARREL**

The Barrel can be plunged into cold water (if avail- **COOLING**
able), to cool it after overheating caused by firing at **THE**
the Emergency Rate, without any injury to the Barrel. **BARREL**

METHOD OF HOLDING BREN GUN (FOR A-A FIRING)

(A) When using the Tripod as A-A Mounting

(*a*) Butt Strap on Shoulder;
(*b*) Left Hand gripping the Carrying Handle;
(*c*) Right Hand on Pistol Grip;
(*d*) Balance Body with Legs well apart.

(B) In Absence of Tripod

The BREN **may** be fired, for short periods, from the **STANDING**
Shoulder, Standing.

Or preferably Kneeling, with Butt resting on Hip. **KNEELING**

Or Sitting down, leaning against a support, with Butt **SITTING**
on the ground.

V

HOTCHKISS GUN NOTES

ORIGIN

Of Austrian origin, this Gun was formerly manufactured by the Hotchkiss Company, of Paris and Coventry. It was used in the French and Belgian Armies. The French authorities preferred the Air-Cooled Hotchkiss to a Water-Cooled Gun, owing to the difficulty of obtaining water in the desert areas where, prior to the War of 1914–18, the French Army did most of its fighting.

CAVALRY AND TANK WEAPON

In the British Army, the Light Hotchkiss Gun was issued to Cavalry Regiments and Tanks, as its shape could more easily be carried on horseback or fitted in Tanks. In the Tank Corps, Belts (of 50 rounds) were used instead of the metal Strips.

PARTICULARS OF THE .303 HOTCHKISS (LIGHT MACHINE) GUN

WEIGHT OF GUN	28 lb.
WEIGHT OF MAGAZINE	1 lb. 15 oz.
(Strip of 30 rounds)	(Filled)
RATE OF FIRE	600 rounds per minute
SINGLE SHOTS	can also be fired

COOLING SYSTEM

AIR COOLED.—The very thick and heavy Barrel is fitted with 25 ring-shaped flanges around the thickest part, thus affording extra space for the air to circulate.

CHANGING THE BARREL

THE BARREL CAN BE CHANGED WHEN OVERHEATED (after 500 rounds have been fired) in approximately 20 seconds.

ENGAGEMENT OF AIR TARGETS BY LIGHT AUTOMATICS

1. *Air Targets*, suitable for Light Automatic Guns (or Rifles), are enemy Airplanes flying at a height of 1,000 feet or under, and at a distance not greater than 600 yards.

Beyond this range the .303 (or .300) S.A.A. bullet will not retain sufficient penetrating power for good Fire Effect.

SUITABLE TARGETS

2. At 600 yards National Markings (of varying shapes and colours) on the Wings of a crossing or overhead Plane *may* be visible. But the colours are not recognisable. Markings on the Tail or Body are invisible.

VISIBILITY OF MARKINGS

Beyond 600 yards the Markings quickly become indistinguishable, and the Aircraft will be seen in silhouette.

At closer ranges the pilot's head, the struts, and the colours of the National Markings soon become visible, and the Nationality of the Plane becomes apparent.

NATIONALITY OF PLANE

3. The general rule is that Fire should be opened directly this maximum range for Small-Arms Weapons is reached. Aiming is easier at 600 yards, and chances of hitting the Target are favourable. But *see also para. 7 (below)*.

OPENING FIRE

4. N.B.—Since opening fire *is likely to disclose to the enemy (for flashes of M.G. or rifle fire are visible to aircraft) the presence of troops in the area over which he is flying*, orders to open fire should not be given when concealment is the first consideration.

CONCEALMENT

5. The Hostile Aircraft may be either:—

  (a) Crossing the Gun's position, or
  (b) Diving to attack it.

The former is likely to provide opportunities for both Light Machine-Gun and Rifle fire. The same principles apply to all Small Arms.

CROSSING TARGETS
6. (a) Easiest at maximum effective range, **Aiming at Crossing Targets** becomes increasingly difficult the nearer the Target passes overhead.

Above an Angle of Sight of 50 degrees Aiming may become impracticable. It is then preferable to stop firing, switch the Gun around, and re-engage the Plane as it flies away. If, however, another enemy Plane approaches, the new Target should be engaged in preference to the receding one.

(b) THE DIVE ATTACK AT THE GUN'S POSITION.

DIVE BOMBERS
The Dive Bomber gives practically no warning, and is either Diving or Climbing Away.

When diving down at the Gun site it is flying straight down the Trajectory (Stream of Tracers), and therefore affords an easy Target. When climbing away it makes an easier Target than when almost overhead.

THE DIVE
The Beginning of the Dive is seen when the Aeroplane banks over to lose height. Fire *may* be opened the moment the Wings begin to tilt.

RESERVING FIRE
7. But in recent fighting against Dive-Bombers, Lewis and Bren Guns have been used with the greatest effect by gunners holding their fire until the very closest ranges have been reached.

INFANTRY ATTACK
N.B.—If enemy Infantry are attacking under cover of a barrage of bombs from his own Planes, L.M.G.'s should not be used against the Aircraft overhead, but must be kept ready for use against the enemy Infantry.

VII

AIMING AND CONTROLLING FIRE BY OBSERVATION OF TRACERS

FIRE CONTROL
Fire is controlled by **observing the Stream of Tracers at or near the Target,** and correcting it on to the Target until hits are obtained.

POINT OF AIM
Point of Aim for Light Machine-Guns (and Rifles) is **12 degrees ahead of Target** for Crossing Aeroplanes, regardless of their speed.

N.B.—For Dive-Bombers, diving directly towards the

Gun's position, **ahead** of Target here means a Point of Aim just **above** the Nose of the Plane.

A rough guide for estimating 12 degrees is:—

WIDTH from 1st to 4th fingers (wide-spread) of left hand, at arm's length.

12 DEGREES

N.B.—This holds good at any range.

---

(1) **Set Sights at 500 yards.** Glance at Sights only to obtain Elevation.

ELEVATION

---

(2) **Direct the Gun with 12 degrees "lead"** in front of Nose of Plane.

AIMING

Swing along Line of Flight and press Trigger.

SWING

SWING must not be checked at moment of pressing the Trigger.

All further use of Sights can now be ignored.

---

(3) **SPEED IN OPENING FIRE IS ESSENTIAL.**
Opening Burst should be on, or close in **FRONT** of, the Target.

SPEED IN OPENING FIRE

Bursts falling **BEHIND** are not only useless, but also are difficult to correct.

---

(4) Short Bursts are ineffective, and the Trigger should be pressed until all the rounds in the Magazine have been expended.

CONTINUOUS FIRE

---

(5) **The firer's EYES should be focussed on the Target,** and **not** on **the Tracers.**

EYES ON TARGET

---

(6) Tracers will now appear in his Field of View, and his Aim can be corrected on to the Target.

TRACERS

---

(7) **Slow down or increase SWING** of Gun according to Observation of the Stream of Tracers seen at the the Nose of the Plane.

TRAVERSE

---

(8) **Tracers missing** will appear to fall **behind** in a long **curved** Trajectory. This is owing to the speed at which the Plane is moving across the path of the Tracer.

TRACERS MISSING

13

The faster the Plane and the longer the range, the greater will this curve appear to be.

TRACERS HITTING

(9) **Tracers hitting** are seen in a straighter Trajectory. Their path is shorter, and the **deceptive curve** disappears. (See Diagrams A and B.)

OBSERVATION OF FIRE

(10) **Observation** must be made entirely from the Stream of Tracers at or near Target, and **not** during their initial flight.

APPROACHING TARGET

(11) **For a Target approaching,** the same principles apply. Tracers **missing** appear to be left behind. **Hits** are seen travelling direct to the Target, and the curved "tail" disappears.

CORRECTING AIM

(12) Rather than allowing Bursts to fall behind the Target (as at C in Diagrams), AIM preferably too far in front (as at A); *correcting with slow traverse** until the Tracer reaches the Nose of the Plane.

CORRECTING ELEVATION

(13) **Elevation** must be corrected immediately the Stream of Tracers indicates *high* (as at B), or *low* (as at D, in Diagrams).

WRONG CORRECTION

(14) If the Stream of Tracers is watched too closely, or during its Initial Flight, the eye tends to focus itself on a point in the Trajectory which is nowhere near the Target. *Hence wrong corrections may be made.*

TRACERS IN MAGAZINE

(15) The **proportion of Tracers** used to Mk. VII S.A.A. varies from 3 to 4 in every 5 rounds. The tendency lately has been to increase the number of Tracers used. Ordinary S.A.A. is inserted only to clear the fouling caused by Tracer Ammunition.

BARRAGE OF BULLETS

* An **Alternative Method** to traversing the Gun is to lay a Barrage of Bullets **ahead** of the Plane, but along its Line of Flight (or in the case of a Dive-Bomber attacking the Gun's position, just *above* its Nose), so that the Plane continues on its course into the Barrage.

Appearance of TRACERS at or near Target:—

* TRACERS MISSING

(A) in front;
(B) high;
(C) behind;
(D) low.

TRACERS HITTING

Leave no **curve** behind, and their trajectory is seen to be shorter and straighter.

* N.B.—The pronounced **curve** of Tracers **missing** (shown in DIAGRAMS (A) and (B) by red lines), is an optical illusion, caused by the high speed of the Target moving across the Line of Sight.

The effect on the eye may be compared with the continuous streak caused by passing a level row of lights at night, as seen from the window of an express train.

OBSERVATION OF TRACERS

Diagrams showing outline of enemy Long-Range
Bomber (viz. Heinkel He, IIIK Mk. Va.), used
to attack shipping in the North Sea.

DIAGRAM (A)—PLANE CROSSING GUN'S POSITION

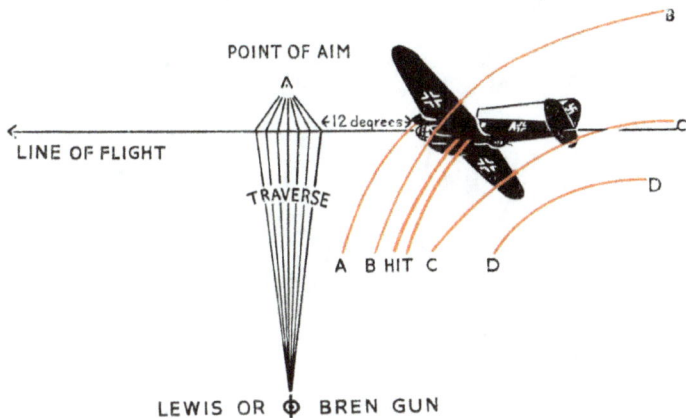

POINT OF AIM

A

←12 degrees→

LINE OF FLIGHT

B

C

D

TRAVERSE

A   B HIT C   D

LEWIS OR ⏀ BREN GUN

DIAGRAM (B)—PLANE APPROACHING DIAGONALLY

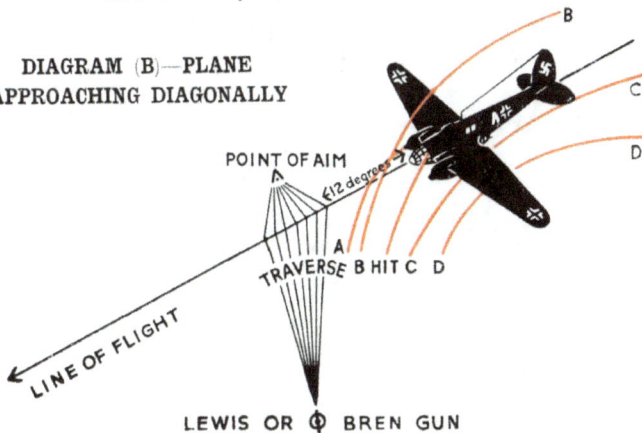

POINT OF AIM

A

←12 degrees→

B

C

D

TRAVERSE B HIT C D

A

LINE OF FLIGHT

LEWIS OR ⏀ BREN GUN

VIII

NOTABLE LEWIS AND BREN GUN SUCCESSES
AGAINST ENEMY AIRCRAFT

Single Lewis and Bren Guns, manned by gunners of the fighting forces on land and sea, the mercantile marine, and trawler flotillas, have been handled with outstanding success, as the following instances (culled from Ministry of Information reports) clearly show:—

(a) *During the withdrawal to the coast* of the Allied Forces in Belgium, in May, 1940.

"A column of French infantry was moving up to the front line when it was attacked by enemy aircraft, with bombs and machine-guns, from a low altitude. The column was obliged to scatter. Each soldier, therefore, had to rely on his own initiative.

LEWIS GUN WITH INFANTRY COLUMN

"One of them, *a private armed with a Lewis Gun,* settled himself at the side of the road and put his gun into position. Then, waiting until one of the German planes dived sufficiently, he took careful aim and *brought it down with his first burst of fire.* Another German plane arrived at full speed, skimming over the ground. Again he took aim, and the second machine fell. This soldier had demonstrated that *an infantryman armed with a Lewis Gun can destroy these formidable machines.*"

(b) *One Bren Gunner drives off eleven Dorniers.*

An epic action by a Lance-Bombardier of the B.E.F., France, was officially described as follows:—

"At 6 a.m. on Sunday, May 12, 1940, eleven Dornier 215 Aircraft flew at a height of about 50 feet very near to the gun position at which this Lance-Bombardier was stationed. The bombers appeared to be about to attack the gun site, since they were flying in line astern formation in the direction of the site. Although a burst of machine-gun fire came from one of the planes, and he was standing quite unprotected by any form of emplacement, the Bombardier *opened fire with his Bren Gun.*

BREN GUN WITH A-A BATTERY

"The approach of the aircraft was thereby turned away from the site, five planes flying away to one side and six to the other. He engaged each plane as it arrived, and one plane appeared to be hit a large number of times. By his exemplary conduct and coolness in action, this N.C.O. set a very high example to the section and saved the gun site."

15

(c) *During the Evacuation of the B.E.F. from Dunkirk.*

LEWIS GUN AT DUNKIRK

A Lewis gunner on a small British ship successfully fought relays of bombers for several hours—as stated by evacuated B.E.F. soldiers at an East Coast port, on May 30, 1940:—

"Every one of us owes his life to that single man," said one of them. "When we reached the coast we were exhausted, having been fighting and marching day and night for several days. A small British ship had come inshore, stern first, as close as she could. Half wading, half swimming, we clambered on board. Then the bombers came. But as they roared towards us *a Lewis gunner astern of the ship replied.*

FOUR BOMBERS BADLY DAMAGED

"Because of the tide we were unable to sail for several hours. *All the time that Lewis Gun was answering.* At least four of the planes were very badly damaged. The bombs were throwing up spray all round us, and making the ship tremble from stem to stern. Towards the end the ammunition began to run low. We took rounds from our own pouches, and spent the time between attacks refilling the Lewis drums. At last we sailed, but it was not until we were a long way away that the Germans ceased attacking. By this time the gunner was almost dropping from fatigue. When we all gathered round and cheered him, I don't think he heard us. Continuous firing had left him temporarily deaf."

(d) *Enemy Aircraft driven off by Fishing Trawlers.*

TRAWLER LEWIS GUNNERS

Now that they have been given arms for defence against air attacks by Nazi planes, fighting enemy Aircraft is a sideline of the men of Britain's fishing fleet.

(i) "A Trawler was fishing peacefully when she was attacked by two German aircraft. The first came very low over the Trawler, and the third hand *opened fire with the Lewis Gun.* His bullets ripped into the plane, and in a matter of seconds it had black smoke pouring from both engines and a trail of dirty white smoke was coming from the fuselage. The aircraft, crippled, tried to fly away to the eastward, but it lost height rapidly and could not climb. It was followed by a second plane, which abandoned its attack on the Trawler when it saw how effectively the fishermen could hit back."

16

(ii) *Trawler Lewis Gunner brings down Heinkel* 111
   Bomber.

"Another fishing vessel, attacked by a Heinkel 111 Bomber, opened *such effective fire with its Lewis Gun* that it brought the attacker crashing down into the sea. The crew of the Heinkel were picked up and are now prisoners in England."

LEWIS GUN DESTROYS HEINKEL BOMBER

(iii) *Chief Engineer of Motor Ship drives off Enemy Bomber.*

"A Goole motor ship was machine-gunned within half an hour of leaving port. The enemy plane had swooped down with engines cut out. Though taken by surprise, the chief engineer leapt to the ship's Lewis Gun, and *poured four drums of ammunition* into the tail of the plane as it made off astern.

ENGINEER AS LEWIS GUNNER

"Tracer bullets were seen entering the tail, and, as the rear gunner never fired a shot, he was probably hit. While the Lewis Gun was firing the plane dived to within a few yards of the surface and then banked and turned. Though bullets penetrated many parts of the ship, there was only one slight casualty aboard the trawler."

(iv) *Fishing Smack versus Torpedo Boat.*

"A fishing smack was carrying 16 German air-force prisoners, some of whom had been in the air only a few hours before. Within a few minutes of putting to sea the ship was shelled by a German torpedo boat. Then the latter fired a torpedo, which missed. The torpedo boat swung to attack again. A running fight developed, but the fishing vessel's *single Lewis Gun* and the rifles of some British soldiers drove off the enemy. Next morning the fishing vessel reached a South Coast port."

TORPEDO BOAT DRIVEN OFF

(e) *Lewis Gunner brings down Enemy Bomber attacking an Aerodrome.*

Useful lessons have been learnt from operations in France on the subject of defending Aerodromes from attack by air-borne troops. In the recent operations south of the Somme it was obvious that attacks by parachutists, and possibly by aeroplane-carried troops, would be made on certain large Aerodromes sited right in the heart of the lines of communication of the B.E.F. at Rouen.

LEWIS GUNS (AND RIFLES) PROTECT AERODROME

"At one Aerodrome the majority of the infantry posted were the personnel of a Divisional H.Q. These included clerks, cooks, drivers, and storemen, armed with their rifles and a few Lewis and Bren guns. As most of the men were old soldiers, the Lewis Guns were particular favourites with them.

"At about five o'clock a most determined attack was made from very low altitudes by about 30 machines. Two or three machines were shot down by small arms and light automatic fire from the troops guarding the Aerodrome.

"SCROUNGED" LEWIS GUN

"One particular aeroplane fell to the lone efforts of a corporal who was in charge of the Divisional H.Q. cook-house. This corporal was a particularly expert Lewis gunner who was firing a Lewis Gun which he had 'scrounged' from no one quite knows where. The aeroplane fell in flames not many yards away from his post. After this attack had been repelled the enemy confined his efforts to bombing from a very high altitude."

———

(f) *Two Heinkel* 115 (*Seaplane*) *Bombers shot down by a single Lewis Gun in* 20 *minutes' fight.*

SINGLE LEWIS GUN DESTROYS TWO SEAPLANES

"On August 2, 1940, the S.S. *Highlander*, of Aberdeen, reached port with wreckage of a Heinkel 115 bomber lying across her broken bridge and after deck. The rest of that Heinkel and the wreckage of another were in the North Sea, *shot down by one Lewis Gun* manned by two gunners.

"The first plane appeared soon after midnight on August 1st. Twice it swooped across the ship, coming lower each time, but the gunner *held his fire* until it came a third time, when he opened fire. This time the plane attacked and dived from bow to stern. The gunner aimed at the spot he judged it would come into sight over the superstructure of the ship. The machine came right into his line of sight as he opened fire. It lurched over the ship about 30 feet away and then crashed. One wing caught the side of the bridge, the other wing fell over the deck and smashed the railings. The body then broke away and bursting into flames crashed into the sea.

"As the crew were looking for survivors, a second Heinkel appeared and dived to the attack. The second gunner persuaded his comrade to hand over the Lewis Gun to him. He also *held his fire* until the plane got really

PLATE III.

LEWIS GUNNERS IN NAVAL SPEED BOATS

Used to patrol inland waterways where enemy Seaplanes might alight in case of invasion.

near. He scored hits with his first burst, and the second
Heinkel crashed straight into the sea. The whole action
was over in 20 minutes."

———

(g) *R.E. Officer brings down Bomber attacking an Airfield.*

"During August, 1940, an officer of the Royal Engi-
neers was in command of a party of sappers working
on the defences of a Sussex airfield, when it was suddenly
attacked by German planes. The officer got into a pill-
box of his own construction, with a *Lewis Gun* in hand.
The planes were swooping down almost to the level of
the chimney pots. He winged one, but determined to
bring down the next. This one, a Dornier, crashed three-
quarters of a mile away. The crew of three were all killed
by Lewis Gun fire, and the officer was officially credited
with the Dornier."

**R.E.
OFFICER
BRINGS
DOWN
DIVE-BOMBER**

———

(h) *A Dornier 17 Bomber brought down by a Bren
Gunner.*

"A corporal operating a *Bren Gun* shot down a big
German bomber, a Dornier 17, carrying a crew of six,
in the early hours of November 8, 1940, at Abberton,
near Colchester. The machine was badly damaged as it
crashed. Two of the crew were taken to hospital. The
other four were made prisoners."

**BREN GUN
DESTROYS
DORNIER
RAIDER**

———

(i) *Norwegian Lewis Gunner destroys German Bomber.*

"It was learned yesterday (February 5, 1941) that a
German bomber which crashed recently in the sea off the
Cornish coast was shot down by a Norwegian merchant
ship. Diving out of the clouds, the bomber dropped four
bombs, which fell in the sea around the vessel, and made
off into the clouds again. A few seconds later it returned
to rake the vessel with machine-gun fire. A Norwegian
sailor stuck to his post at a Lewis Gun, hit the raider,
causing it to dive, and then riddled it with bullets as it
was coming down. The crew of four were killed."

**NORWEGIAN
SAILOR
DESTROYS
BOMBER**